HEROES OF HISTORY

WARRIORS

Written by Anita Ganeri
Illustrated by Joe Todd Stanton

PowerKiDS press

Published in 2026 by The Rosen Publishing Group, Inc.
2544 Clinton Street, Buffalo, NY 14224

Created by:
Author: Anita Ganeri
Additional text: Nicola Barber
Illustrator: Joe Todd Stanton
Additional Illustrations: Katie Abey
Editorial: Hannah Wilson, Lydia Halliday
Senior Designer: Krina Patel
Designer: Natasha Rees
Index: Vanessa Bird

Cataloging-in-Publication Data

Names: Ganeri, Anita, 1961, author. | Todd-Stanton, Joe, illustrator.

Title: Warriors / by Anita Ganeri, illustrated by Joe Todd-Stanton.

Description: Buffalo, NY : PowerKids Press, 2026. | Series: Heroes of history | Includes glossary and index.

Identifiers: ISBN 9781499454994 (pbk.) | ISBN 9781499455007 (library bound) | ISBN 9781499455014 (ebook)

Subjects: LCSH: Military biography--Juvenile literature.

Classification: LCC U51.G364 2026 | DDC 355.0092'2--dc23

Manufactured in the United States of America

CPSIA Compliance Information: Batch #CSPK26. For further information contact Rosen Publishing at 1-800-237-9932.

CONTENTS

INTRODUCTION

History is packed with heroes and heroines who left a lasting legacy behind. Some were larger-than-life characters, born leaders who inspired their followers. Others worked away quietly, shunning the limelight. They earned their fame in different ways - through hard work, determination and, sometimes, sheer luck.

WARRIORS

Throughout history, great warriors have found themselves pitted against each other in bitter battles and conflicts. With bravery and self-sacrifice, they have faced danger, disaster, and even death. Some warriors have fought in armies, guarding their lords or kings, bound together by codes of loyalty, courage, and respect.

Sir William Marshal

Joan of Arc

Some fought to defend their beliefs, often against huge odds, while others battled for the freedom of their people or country. Many did not fear death as long as it was honorable.

In this chapter, you can read about a dashing knight famed for his fighting skills and chivalry, a brave fighter who gave up her own life for her faith, a Samurai from a humble home who rose to become a great hero, and an Apache who suffered a terrible tragedy and vowed to take his revenge.

Saigo Takamori

Geronimo

Sir William Marshal

Medieval Knight

In medieval times, knights were dashing soldiers, bound by a code of chivalry to fight for their country and protect their king or lord. Among them was William Marshal, who rose from humble beginnings to become the greatest knight Europe had ever seen.

Early life

Born in 1146, William Marshal had an exciting start to life. As a young boy, he was taken hostage by King Stephen to force William's father (who was fighting for Stephen's rival, Queen Matilda) to surrender his castle. The king threatened to have William hanged if his father did not obey. But his threat did not work. So King Stephen ordered his men to launch William from a trebuchet (giant catapult), but in the end he could not bring himself to harm the boy.

Becoming a knight

William's father was a nobleman, but because William was not the eldest son and had no lands or fortune to inherit, he had to make his own way in life. It was decided that he would become a knight. At the age of 12, he was sent to Normandy in France to be brought up in the household of William de Tancarville (his mother's cousin). He began his training, learning not only swordsmanship and riding, but also Latin, chivalry, and how to cope with the politics of a life at court.

William was knighted in 1166 while on campaign in Normandy. His first experience of battle is said to have been a success. According to reports, William fought bravely, but he did not manage to seize any booty or hostages to ransom off. For a knight, making a profit was just as important as fighting with honor. But he was soon to find his real talent in life — winning tournaments.

SIR WILL'S KNIGHTLY DIARY

Sometime in 1167
Normandy, France

A brilliant day! Lord William took me to my first tournament. I won everything, including most of the battles (which were as deadly as the real thing). And this time, I remembered to take the losing knights hostage, so I made loads of money ransoming them off with their horses and armor. This is definitely the life for me.

Summer 1168
Poitiers, France

Things haven't been going so well lately. In March, my lord was killed in a skirmish, and I was taken prisoner. I had a wound in my leg that turned nasty. Luckily, someone took pity on me and sent me some bandages, hidden inside a loaf of bread. That saved my life. Anyway, eventually the ransom was paid by Queen Eleanor of Aquitaine – apparently, she'd been impressed by my bravery.

A day in August 1189
Tower of London, England
My wedding day! My new wife, Isabel de Clare, is beautiful, kind . . . and really, really rich. Her father is the Earl of Pembroke and he's given us several large estates as wedding presents. I'm going to be one of the wealthiest men in the kingdom — who'd have thought it? Now we've just got to decide which one of our (many) castles we should live in.

June 15, 1215
Runnymede, England
For the last few years, I've been mostly in France, negotiating on behalf of King John. Then King John and I fell out big time (long story). Anyway, I'm back in favor, and I'm here at Runnymede to witness the sealing of the Magna Carta. It's a charter setting out new laws that everyone, including the king, has to obey — let's see how that turns out.

November 11, 1216
Gloucester, England
King John died in October and I organized his funeral and burial in Worcester Cathedral. A sad day. Today, I was named as regent for his son, King Henry II. He's only nine years old so he needs some help ruling the kingdom. A very great honor indeed.

MILITARY LEADERS

Sir William Marshal had all the best qualities of a knight. Like many knights, he was a skilled horseman and a fierce fighter, and he was also brave and loyal.

Engraving of a medieval English knight

The greatest knight

William Marshal, the son of a nobleman of little importance, ended up as regent — effectively the ruler of England. At the age of 70, he led the king's army into battle and victory over the rebellious barons. After his death in 1219, he was called the "greatest knight that ever lived."

William the Conqueror

William became Duke of Normandy (in France) as a young boy and grew up to be a skilled knight. In 1066, he invaded England and won the Battle of Hastings. William was crowned king of England on Christmas Day.

Bayeux Tapestry showing Norman invasion

Statue of Díaz on his horse, Babieca

Rodrigo Díaz de Vivar

Rodrigo Díaz de Vivar, a nobleman from Castile, northern Spain, became commander of the royal troops at an early age. Later, he became military leader for the Muslim rulers of Zaragoza — a kingdom in northeastern Spain. He conquered the kingdom of Valencia, ruling it until his death in 1099.

Timeline of medieval army commanders

1066

William the Conqueror

French duke wins the Battle of Hastings and becomes King William I of England.

1094

Rodrigo Díaz de Vivar

Castilian nobleman, nicknamed "El Cid" (meaning "the Lord"), conquers Valencia.

1191

Richard the Lionheart

English king joins the Third Crusade, a campaign to seize control of the Holy Land, an area now part of the Middle East.

1217

Sir William Marshal

At the age of 70, leads the king's army to victory at the Battle of Lincoln.

1242

Alexander Nevsky

Prince of Novgorod (now part of Russia) conquers the Germans in the Battle of the Ice, fought on a frozen lake.

Joan of Arc

Faith Fighter

The Hundred Years War between France and England lasted from 1337 to 1453 (actually 116 years). The soldiers were fighting for control of France. Among them was an unlikely heroine — a young girl called Joan, who claimed that God had sent her to save France.

War-torn times

At the time of Joan's birth on January 6, 1412, the Hundred Years War had already been raging for 75 years. At stake was the question of which country — England or France — had the right to the French crown. Nearly all of the fighting had taken place in France as a series of wars, with short periods of peace in between. By now, the French army had not won any major victories for many years and the English had the upper hand.

Joan, the daughter of a farmer, was born in the village of Domrémy in northeastern France. She did not learn to read or write, but her mother took her to church and taught her about her Christian faith and this became a guiding light in Joan's life.

During Joan's childhood, her village was attacked several times — and even set on fire — but it still remained loyal to the French crown. Then, in 1420, the French queen, Catherine of Valois, signed a peace treaty, disinheriting her son Charles (later Charles VII) and making the English king, Henry V, ruler of both England and France.

His young son, Henry VI, succeeded him in 1422. England occupied much of northern France, and many people in Joan's village were forced to flee. Then, one day, Joan's life changed forever, and with it the fate of France.

JOAN OF ARC'S ORLÉANS DIARY

One day in 1425
Domrémy, France

An amazing thing has happened. I was in the garden when three figures appeared in front of me. I knew them from pictures in church — they were St. Michael, St. Catherine, and St. Margaret, sent by God to me! I cried because they were so beautiful. They told me that I must save France by helping to drive out the English and making Prince Charles king. Then they were gone. I still can't believe it.

Sometime in early 1429
Orléans, France

I'm here at the royal court, though getting here wasn't easy. I had to crop my hair and put on boys' clothes so no one knew I was a girl because there's a stupid rule that says only boys are allowed to fight. Then I had to cross enemy territory, which took 11 days. I knew Charles as soon as I saw him and told him he would be crowned soon. I also told him that God wanted me to lead an army to Orléans, which is under seige from the English. And guess what? He agreed!

May 8, 1429
Orléans, France

It's over. The siege is over after five long months. The turning point came yesterday. I rode into battle, carrying my banner, but an arrow hit me in the shoulder and I had to turn back. I came back later for another assault and we were able to capture the English fortress. After this, the English left in a hurry. I'm being called a hero, but this is all God's work.

July 17, 1429
Reims, France

The day we've all been waiting for — Prince Charles' coronation in the cathedral. He is now officially King Charles VII of France. Long live the king!

Spring 1430
Rouen Castle, France

I'm being kept prisoner by the English. While we were defending Compiègne, I was thrown from my horse and captured. They tell me they're putting me on trial for witchcraft and heresy, among many other things. I've been trying to get a message to the king, but so far he's not replied. I spend my days praying — only God can help me now.

DETERMINED DEVOTEES

Joan of Arc believed that she had been called by God to go into battle. Many other people throughout history have been prepared to lay down their lives for the sake of their faith.

Statue of Joan of Arc

Joan the saint

Joan of Arc was put on trial by the English, accused of being a witch, of heresy, and of dressing like a man. King Charles could not help, and so Joan was found guilty. On May 30, 1431, she was burned to death at the stake. Joan was made a Catholic saint in 1920.

Thomas Becket

Thomas Becket worked for the Archbishop of Canterbury and became friends with King Henry II. In 1161, Henry made Becket archbishop. But Becket argued with the king and stood up for the Church. In 1170, he was murdered.

Cathedral window honouring Becket

Syrian banknote depicting Saladin

Saladin

Saladin was the sultan of Egypt and Syria, and the founder of the Ayyubid dynasty, which ruled much of the Middle East in the late 1100s and 1200s. A devoted Muslim, Saladin conquered the Christian Crusaders in 1187 to retake Jerusalem. Saladin gave much of his money to the poor.

Timeline of faith fighters

1099

Godfrey of Bouillon

Medieval knight becomes Defender of the Holy Sepulchre after the capture of Jerusalem during the First Crusade.

1170

Thomas Becket

Murdered in Canterbury Cathedral after opposing King Henry II.

1187

Saladin

Muslim leader recaptures Jerusalem from the Crusaders after a famous victory at the Battle of Hattin.

1430

Joan of Arc

Captured by the English, accused of witchcraft, and burnt at the stake one year later.

1535

Thomas More

Beheaded for treason for opposing King Henry VIII's separation from the Catholic Church.

SAIGO TAKAMORI

Samurai

Traditional Japanese warriors — Samurai — were bound by a strict code of honor: the Bushido or "Way of the Warrior." The code valued loyalty, bravery, and respect, all virtues that Saigo Takamori, known as the Last Samurai, possessed in abundance.

Early life

Saigo was born on January 23, 1828 in Kagoshima, Japan. His father was a low-ranking Samurai, but the family were still poor and only just managed to scrape by. Saigo and his six younger brothers and sisters shared one blanket at night, and his parents had to borrow money to buy land to grow food for the family.

At the age of six, Saigo was sent to the local Samurai school, where he was given his first sword. It was his first step on the road to becoming a great warrior, though he preferred reading to practicing sword fighting. Saigo left school at the age of 14, and went into the service of the local daimyo (lord). Some time later, he got married, but tragedy was not far off. Both of his parents died within months of each other, leaving Saigo head of a large family, with very little money to support them.

Promotion and exile

At work, Saigo's talents were quickly recognized and he was promoted to the post of the daimyo's attendant. Together, they travelled to Edo, the capital of the shogun (military ruler), where Saigo became the daimyo's closest advisor. He secretly helped the lord to plot with his allies to put the emperor back in power, at the expense of the shogun.

On July 16, 1858, the daimyo died suddenly and Saigo found his life in danger as the shogun threatened to kill anyone who had supported the emperor. Saigo fled to Kagoshima, but the new daimyo would not protect him. Rather than face arrest, Saigo went into exile on a small island. There, he got married again, had a son, and carved out a new life for himself.

SAIGO'S SAMURAI DIARY

February 1864
Kyoto, Japan
What an exciting few years! There I was in exile, when I was suddenly called back to Kyoto and offered a position in the emperor's court. It didn't last long. I soon fell foul of the new daimyo and was banished to a small island. Again. Worse was to come. I was moved to an even smaller island — basically a lump of rock in the sea — where I stayed for a year. Anyway, I'm back now, in Kyoto, where I've been appointed Commander of the Imperial Army. No one is more surprised than me.

April 4, 1868
Edo, Japan
A great day. After weeks of hard fighting, the shogun (who doesn't want the emperor back in power) has surrendered. Phew! After a fierce battle at Toba-Fushimi, we beat him back to Edo and had him surrounded so he didn't have much choice. But I'm glad it's over. We allowed him to keep his head — there's already been enough bloodshed.

October 1873
Kagoshima, Japan

That's it — I've resigned. I've had enough of all the fighting. I'm retiring to the country to play with my kids and go fishing. The final straw was the business with Korea. The Koreans wouldn't accept the emperor as, well, the emperor, and this was a terrible insult to Japan. The government wouldn't invade Korea despite this. I tried to persuade them that it was a reason to go to war — but no one took a blind bit of notice. Now, where's my fishing rod?

February 1877
Kumamoto Castle, near Kagoshima

Well, that didn't last for long. I'm holed up in Kumamoto Castle with an army of rebel Samurai. We didn't like the way the government was taking away our privileges — including stopping us from carrying swords — so I was asked to lead a protest against the government. To be honest, it's not going that well. We're massively outnumbered by the emperor's army and we're running short of supplies.

September 23, 1877
Shiroyama mountain, near Kagoshima

We can't go on much longer. There are only 300 of us left and tomorrow we go into battle against 7,000 imperial troops. I'm not afraid of dying, as long as I die an honorable death. That is the way of the Samurai.

BRAVE WARRIORS

Saigo died at the Battle of Shiroyama, but his reputation as a legendary hero lived on in Japan. Like other great warriors in history, he is remembered for his bravery and skill.

Statue of Saigo in Tokyo, Japan

The last samurai

The Battle of Shiroyama was the last stand for the Samurai rebels. During the attack, Saigo was seriously wounded, so one of his servants beheaded him — giving him a Samurai's honorable death. Saigo is known today as the "Last Samurai."

Alexander the Great

Aged 20, Alexander became king of Macedonia and began conquering territories that were under the rule of the Persian Empire. By 331 BCE, he controlled a huge empire that extended from the Adriatic Sea to the Indus River.

Alexander in battle

Stamp depicting Zenobia

Zenobia

Zenobia became queen of the Palmyrene Empire (based in Syria) in 267 CE and led her armies to conquer Egypt. But when the Roman emperor defeated the Palmyreans, Zenobia was taken to Rome. No one knows what happened to her, and the rest of her life remains a mystery.

Timeline of skilled fighters

336 BCE
Alexander the Great
Comes to the throne in Macedonia and becomes one of the greatest military commanders in history.

269 CE
Zenobia
Queen of the Palmyrene Empire challenges Roman rule in Egypt.

1013
Sweyn Forkbeard
Viking king of Denmark becomes the first Danish king of England.

1071
Alp Arslan
"Courageous Lion" and second sultan of the Seljuk Empire defeats the Byzantines at the Battle of Manzikert.

1877
Saigo Takamori
Dies an honorable Samurai death at the Battle of Shiroyama.

GERONIMO

Apache Attacker

It used to be traditional for skydivers and paratroopers to shout "GERONIMO!" as they jumped out of an airplane, to show that they were not afraid. But who was the real-life Geronimo and why would calling his name help a person to feel brave?

The early years

Geronimo was born in June 1829 near Turkey Creek, a branch of the Gila River in the modern-day state of Arizona. Back then, Arizona was part of Mexico. His grandfather, Mahko, had been chief of the Chiricahua Apache tribe. Named "Goyahkla" ("one who yawns") by his parents, he would later gain fame as "Geronimo," the greatest Apache warrior of all time.

Young Geronimo dreamed of the day when he would become a great warrior. He practiced his warrior skills with his friends, fighting mock battles and hiding from the enemy, knowing that one day their lives might depend on these skills. Meanwhile, he worked as a farmer, helping his father to tend their crops. It was a traditional Apache upbringing. Geronimo and his family lived in a home made from antelope and deer hides. As soon as Geronimo could handle a bow and arrow, he began to hunt small animals.

A young fighter is born

Aged 17, Geronimo joined the council of warriors, which meant that he could now go into battle. He also earned the right to marry. He had fallen in love with a beautiful girl called Alope. Soon, they married, settled down, and had three children, but his life was about to change forever.

Tension was growing between the Apache and the Mexicans, who accused the Apache of raiding their towns. The Mexican leader, Colonel José María Carrasco, believed that all of the Apache were robbers and murderers. He vowed to take revenge. In March 1851, while Geronimo and the other Apache men were away, he ordered his men to attack the camp where their families lived.

GERONIMO'S APACHE DIARY

March 5, 1858
Kas-ki-yeh, New Mexico

The worst day. We were camping near Kas-ki-yeh. I went into town with the other men to trade. On our way back, we met some people who told us that the Mexicans had attacked our camp. We split up and hid until nightfall when we crept into the camp. Dead bodies lay everywhere, among them my mother, wife, and three little children. From this day on, I vow to get my revenge on the Mexicans, however long it might take and whatever the cost.

Sometime in 1873 (possibly)
Casa Grande, New Mexico

I always knew the Mexicans were a rotten lot, but this time they've gone too far. We were exhausted after months of fighting and so agreed to meet them at Casa Grande to sign a peace treaty. All went well until the Mexicans gave us a drink to celebrate and we all got horribly drunk. Then they killed 20 Apache and captured many more. Peace? Pah! Dirty double-crossers.

Sometime in 1876 (probably)
San Carlos, Arizona

Yes, we're back at the San Carlos Reservation. Those pesky U.S. troops keep rounding us up and bringing us back, as if we're cattle. Anyway, it'll give us time to get more warriors together, and to trade for new guns and ammunition. Then those Mexicans had better watch out!

Sometime in 1880 (possibly)
Robledo Mountains, New Mexico

Hah! That showed them. We escaped from the reservation, but the soldiers came after us, so we hid in a cave in the mountains. They waited outside to catch us . . . and waited, and waited, and waited. While they were waiting, we sneaked out through a secret exit and escaped! They were furious when they found out — serves them right!

September 4, 1886
Skeleton Canyon, Arizona

Another bad day. After years of giving the U.S. authorities the slip, we finally got caught. We just ran out of places to run. I, the great Geronimo, surrendered. There was nothing else I could do! We were taken prisoner and sent to Fort Sam Houston, then to Fort Pickens. They're setting us to work sawing logs, but that won't stop us. No way!

INDEPENDENCE FIGHTERS

After his death, Geronimo's name became linked with daring and courage — it even became the motto of a U.S. Army parachute regiment. Other rebels are also remembered for their bravery.

Photograph of Geronimo taken in 1903

Celebrity and death

In his old age, Geronimo was famous, taking part in many wild west shows, but he was never allowed to return to the land of his birth. In February 1909, he fell from his horse and died a few weeks later. On his deathbed, he confessed that he regretted surrendering in 1886.

Boudica

In 60 CE, Boudica, queen of the Iceni, a tribe of eastern England, led a rebellion against the Romans, who had conquered southern Britain. She destroyed Colchester, St. Albans, and London before being defeated.

Statue of Boudica in London

Nanjing's city gate, built under Zhu's rule

Zhu Yuanzhang

Zhu Yuanzhang joined a monastery at a young age. When it was destroyed by Yuan troops, Zhu joined a rebel group fighting to overthrow the ruling Yuan Dynasty, and he soon became a commander. He conquered Nanjing and, in 1368, proclaimed himself emperor of China.

Timeline of bold rebels

60 CE
Boudica
Queen of the Iceni tribe leads a revolt against the Romans in Britain.

1297
William Wallace
Scottish landowner leads a rebellion against the English king and wins a famous victory at Stirling Bridge.

1368
Zhu Yuanzhang
Becomes the first emperor of China's Ming Dynasty.

1813
Simón Bolívar
Venezuelan statesman begins to lead Venezuela, Colombia, Ecuador, Peru, and Bolivia to independence.

1886
Geronimo
Apache warrior surrenders to U.S. authorities.

GLOSSARY

chivalry The system, spirit, ways, or customs of knighthood.

exile An act of being forced to leave one's country or home.

heresy Religious opinion that is opposed to the doctrines of a church.

Magna Carta A charter of liberties that English barons forced King John to sign in June 1215 at Runnymede.

negotiate To discuss something formally in order to reach an agreement.

paratrooper A soldier trained to parachute from an airplane.

reservation Land set aside by the U.S. government for specific Native American tribes to live on.

FOR MORE INFORMATION

Doyle, Abby Badach. *Geronimo.* Buffalo, NY: Enslow Publishing, 2022.

Yomtov, Nel. *How to Be a Samurai.* North Mankato, MN: Pebble Books, 2025.

Biography: Joan of Arc
www.ducksters.com/biography/women_leaders/joan_of_arc.php

INDEX